50 Japan's Winter Comfort Food

By: Kelly Johnson

Table of Contents

- Oden (Simmered Fish Cakes and Vegetables)
- Nabe (Hot Pot)
- Sukiyaki (Sweet Soy Sauce Hot Pot)
- Shabu-Shabu (Thinly Sliced Meat Hot Pot)
- Yudofu (Hot Simmered Tofu)
- Tonjiru (Pork and Miso Soup)
- Zenzai (Sweet Red Bean Soup with Mochi)
- Nikujaga (Meat and Potato Stew)
- Chanko Nabe (Sumo Wrestler's Hot Pot)
- Hōtō (Thick Flat Noodles in Miso Broth)
- Ankake Ramen (Thickened Soy Sauce Broth Ramen)
- Buta Kimchi Nabe (Pork and Kimchi Hot Pot)
- Curry Udon (Thick Udon in Curry Broth)
- Katsudon (Pork Cutlet Rice Bowl)
- Unagi Hitsumabushi (Grilled Eel Over Rice)
- Shio Ramen (Salt-Flavored Ramen)
- Miso Ramen (Hokkaido-Style Ramen)
- Ebi Chiri (Spicy Chili Shrimp)
- Gyoza Nabe (Dumpling Hot Pot)
- Omurice (Omelette Rice)
- Okayu (Japanese Rice Porridge)
- Nabeyaki Udon (Hot Udon Noodle Soup)
- Mochi Gratin (Baked Cheesy Mochi)
- Crab Nabe (Snow Crab Hot Pot)
- Motsunabe (Offal Hot Pot)
- Yakiimo (Roasted Sweet Potatoes)
- Fugu Nabe (Blowfish Hot Pot)
- Kamameshi (Iron Pot Rice)
- Kinoko Gohan (Mushroom Rice)
- Hokkaido Butter Corn Ramen (Creamy Corn Ramen)
- Zōsui (Rice Porridge from Hot Pot Broth)
- Salmon Chan-Chan Yaki (Miso-Grilled Salmon)
- Hiyayakko (Cold Tofu with Toppings)
- Anago Meshi (Grilled Saltwater Eel Rice)
- Gindara Saikyo Yaki (Miso-Marinated Black Cod)

- Tofu Steak (Pan-Seared Tofu in Sauce)
- Oyakodon (Chicken and Egg Rice Bowl)
- Takikomi Gohan (Seasoned Mixed Rice)
- Buri Daikon (Simmered Yellowtail and Daikon)
- Nikuman (Steamed Meat Buns)
- Yosenabe (Mixed Hot Pot)
- Imoni (Taro and Beef Stew)
- Tamago Zake (Egg and Sake Drink)
- Kiritanpo (Grilled Rice Skewers)
- Satsuma Jiru (Pork and Sweet Potato Soup)
- Kinako Mochi (Toasted Soybean Flour-Covered Mochi)
- Anmitsu (Winter Dessert with Red Beans and Jelly)
- Yuba Soba (Tofu Skin Soba Noodles)
- Hakusai Itame (Stir-Fried Napa Cabbage)
- Dorayaki (Red Bean Pancakes)

Oden (Simmered Fish Cakes and Vegetables)

Ingredients

- 4 cups dashi broth
- 2 tbsp soy sauce
- 1 tbsp mirin
- 1 tbsp sake
- Assorted fish cakes
- Daikon, sliced
- Boiled eggs
- Konnyaku, sliced

Instructions

1. Simmer dashi, soy sauce, mirin, and sake.
2. Add fish cakes, daikon, eggs, and konnyaku.
3. Simmer for 1 hour and serve warm.

Nabe (Hot Pot)

Ingredients

- 4 cups dashi broth
- 2 tbsp soy sauce
- 1 tbsp mirin
- 200g thinly sliced meat (beef, pork, or chicken)
- 1/2 cup mushrooms
- 1/2 cup napa cabbage
- 1/4 cup tofu, cubed

Instructions

1. Heat dashi, soy sauce, and mirin in a pot.
2. Add meat, mushrooms, cabbage, and tofu.
3. Simmer until cooked and serve.

Sukiyaki (Sweet Soy Sauce Hot Pot)

Ingredients

- 200g thinly sliced beef
- 1/2 cup tofu, cubed
- 1/2 cup mushrooms
- 1/2 cup napa cabbage
- 1/4 cup green onions, chopped
- 2 tbsp soy sauce
- 1 tbsp sugar
- 1 tbsp mirin
- 1 raw egg (for dipping)

Instructions

1. Heat soy sauce, sugar, and mirin in a pot.
2. Add beef, tofu, mushrooms, and cabbage.
3. Cook until done and dip into raw egg before eating.

Shabu-Shabu (Thinly Sliced Meat Hot Pot)

Ingredients

- 4 cups kombu dashi broth
- 200g thinly sliced beef or pork
- 1/2 cup mushrooms
- 1/2 cup napa cabbage
- 1/4 cup tofu, cubed
- Ponzu sauce (for dipping)

Instructions

1. Heat dashi in a pot.
2. Dip meat into broth briefly until cooked.
3. Serve with ponzu sauce.

Yudofu (Hot Simmered Tofu)

Ingredients

- 4 cups kombu dashi broth
- 1 block tofu, cubed
- 1/4 cup green onions, sliced
- 1 tbsp soy sauce

Instructions

1. Heat dashi in a pot.
2. Add tofu and simmer for 5 minutes.
3. Serve with soy sauce and green onions.

Tonjiru (Pork and Miso Soup)

Ingredients

- 4 cups dashi broth
- 100g pork belly, sliced
- 1/2 cup daikon, sliced
- 1/2 cup carrots, sliced
- 1 tbsp miso paste
- 1/4 cup green onions

Instructions

1. Simmer pork, daikon, and carrots in dashi.
2. Stir in miso paste.
3. Garnish with green onions and serve.

Zenzai (Sweet Red Bean Soup with Mochi)

Ingredients

- 1/2 cup azuki beans, soaked overnight
- 3 cups water
- 1/4 cup sugar
- 2 mochi pieces

Instructions

1. Boil beans until soft, then add sugar.
2. Grill mochi until slightly crispy.
3. Serve warm with mochi.

Nikujaga (Meat and Potato Stew)

Ingredients

- 200g thinly sliced beef or pork
- 2 potatoes, cubed
- 1/2 onion, sliced
- 1 cup dashi broth
- 2 tbsp soy sauce
- 1 tbsp sugar

Instructions

1. Simmer dashi, soy sauce, and sugar in a pot.
2. Add meat, potatoes, and onion.
3. Cook until potatoes are soft.

Chanko Nabe (Sumo Wrestler's Hot Pot)

Ingredients

- 4 cups chicken broth
- 200g chicken meatballs or sliced chicken
- 1/2 cup tofu, cubed
- 1/2 cup napa cabbage
- 1/2 cup mushrooms
- 1/4 cup green onions

Instructions

1. Heat chicken broth in a pot.
2. Add chicken, tofu, cabbage, and mushrooms.
3. Simmer until cooked and serve hot.

Hōtō (Thick Flat Noodles in Miso Broth)

Ingredients

- 4 cups dashi broth
- 2 tbsp miso paste
- 200g hōtō noodles (or thick udon noodles)
- 1/2 cup pumpkin, sliced
- 1/2 cup napa cabbage, chopped
- 1/4 cup green onions, chopped

Instructions

1. Simmer dashi broth and miso paste.
2. Add pumpkin and cabbage, cooking until soft.
3. Add noodles and simmer for 5 minutes.
4. Serve garnished with green onions.

Ankake Ramen (Thickened Soy Sauce Broth Ramen)

Ingredients

- 3 cups chicken broth
- 2 tbsp soy sauce
- 1 tbsp mirin
- 1 tbsp cornstarch (mixed with 2 tbsp water)
- 200g ramen noodles
- 1/2 cup mixed vegetables (carrot, mushroom, bok choy)

Instructions

1. Simmer chicken broth, soy sauce, and mirin.
2. Stir in cornstarch mixture to thicken the broth.
3. Cook ramen noodles and serve in the broth.
4. Add vegetables and serve.

Buta Kimchi Nabe (Pork and Kimchi Hot Pot)

Ingredients

- 4 cups dashi broth
- 200g pork belly, sliced
- 1/2 cup kimchi
- 1/2 cup tofu, cubed
- 1/4 cup mushrooms
- 1/2 tbsp soy sauce

Instructions

1. Simmer dashi broth and soy sauce.
2. Add pork, kimchi, tofu, and mushrooms.
3. Simmer until cooked and serve hot.

Curry Udon (Thick Udon in Curry Broth)

Ingredients

- 3 cups dashi broth
- 2 tbsp Japanese curry roux
- 1 tbsp soy sauce
- 200g udon noodles
- 100g thinly sliced beef

Instructions

1. Simmer dashi broth and dissolve curry roux.
2. Add soy sauce and beef, cooking until done.
3. Cook udon noodles and serve in curry broth.

Katsudon (Pork Cutlet Rice Bowl)

Ingredients

- 1 pork cutlet (tonkatsu), fried
- 1/2 onion, sliced
- 1/2 cup dashi broth
- 1 tbsp soy sauce
- 1 tbsp mirin
- 1 egg, beaten
- 1 bowl cooked rice

Instructions

1. Simmer dashi, soy sauce, mirin, and onion.
2. Place fried pork cutlet in the pan and pour beaten egg over it.
3. Cook until egg is slightly set, then serve over rice.

Unagi Hitsumabushi (Grilled Eel Over Rice)

Ingredients

- 1 grilled eel fillet (unagi kabayaki)
- 1 bowl cooked rice
- 1 tbsp unagi sauce
- 1/2 tbsp green onions, chopped

Instructions

1. Slice grilled eel into small strips.
2. Serve eel over rice and drizzle with unagi sauce.
3. Garnish with green onions.

Shio Ramen (Salt-Flavored Ramen)

Ingredients

- 4 cups chicken broth
- 1 tbsp salt
- 1 tsp soy sauce
- 200g thin ramen noodles
- 1 boiled egg, halved
- Green onions, sliced

Instructions

1. Simmer chicken broth with salt and soy sauce.
2. Cook ramen noodles and serve in the broth.
3. Top with a boiled egg and green onions.

Miso Ramen (Hokkaido-Style Ramen)

Ingredients

- 4 cups chicken broth
- 2 tbsp miso paste
- 1 tbsp soy sauce
- 200g thick ramen noodles
- 1/2 cup corn kernels
- 1 tbsp butter

Instructions

1. Simmer chicken broth with miso paste and soy sauce.
2. Cook ramen noodles and serve in the broth.
3. Top with corn and butter.

Ebi Chiri (Spicy Chili Shrimp)

Ingredients

- 200g shrimp, peeled and deveined
- 1 tbsp soy sauce
- 1 tbsp chili sauce
- 1 tbsp ketchup
- 1 clove garlic, minced
- 1 tbsp vegetable oil

Instructions

1. Heat oil in a pan and sauté garlic.
2. Add shrimp and stir-fry until pink.
3. Mix soy sauce, chili sauce, and ketchup, then pour over shrimp.
4. Cook for 2 minutes and serve.

Gyoza Nabe (Dumpling Hot Pot)

Ingredients

- 4 cups dashi broth
- 6 gyoza dumplings
- 1/2 cup napa cabbage, chopped
- 1/4 cup mushrooms

Instructions

1. Simmer dashi broth in a pot.
2. Add gyoza, cabbage, and mushrooms.
3. Simmer until dumplings are cooked and serve.

Omurice (Omelette Rice)

Ingredients

- 1 cup cooked rice
- 1/4 cup chicken, diced
- 1 tbsp ketchup
- 1 egg, beaten
- 1 tbsp butter

Instructions

1. Sauté chicken with butter, then add rice and ketchup.
2. In a separate pan, cook beaten egg into an omelet.
3. Place omelet over the rice and serve.

Okayu (Japanese Rice Porridge)

Ingredients

- 1/2 cup short-grain rice
- 3 cups water or dashi broth
- 1/2 tsp salt
- 1 green onion, chopped (for garnish)
- Umeboshi (pickled plum) (optional)

Instructions

1. Rinse rice and add it to a pot with water or dashi.
2. Simmer on low heat for 30–40 minutes, stirring occasionally.
3. Add salt and stir.
4. Serve warm, topped with green onions and umeboshi if desired.

Nabeyaki Udon (Hot Udon Noodle Soup)

Ingredients

- 4 cups dashi broth
- 2 tbsp soy sauce
- 1 tbsp mirin
- 200g udon noodles
- 1/2 cup mushrooms (shiitake, enoki)
- 1/2 cup napa cabbage
- 1 egg
- 1 piece tempura shrimp

Instructions

1. Simmer dashi, soy sauce, and mirin in a pot.
2. Add mushrooms, cabbage, and udon noodles.
3. Crack an egg into the broth and cook until slightly set.
4. Serve topped with tempura shrimp.

Mochi Gratin (Baked Cheesy Mochi)

Ingredients

- 2 mochi pieces
- 1/2 cup heavy cream
- 1/4 cup shredded cheese (cheddar, mozzarella)
- 1/2 tsp soy sauce
- 1/4 tsp black pepper

Instructions

1. Preheat oven to 375°F (190°C).
2. Place mochi in a small baking dish.
3. Pour cream over the mochi and sprinkle with cheese.
4. Bake for 10–15 minutes until bubbly and golden brown.
5. Drizzle with soy sauce and sprinkle with black pepper before serving.

Crab Nabe (Snow Crab Hot Pot)

Ingredients

- 4 cups dashi broth
- 200g snow crab legs
- 1/2 cup napa cabbage
- 1/2 cup mushrooms
- 1/4 cup tofu, cubed
- 1 tbsp soy sauce

Instructions

1. Simmer dashi broth with soy sauce.
2. Add crab legs, cabbage, mushrooms, and tofu.
3. Cook for 10 minutes until crab is fully heated.
4. Serve hot.

Motsunabe (Offal Hot Pot)

Ingredients

- 4 cups dashi broth
- 200g beef or pork offal, cleaned
- 1/2 cup napa cabbage
- 1/2 cup garlic chives
- 1 tbsp soy sauce
- 1 clove garlic, minced

Instructions

1. Simmer dashi broth with soy sauce and garlic.
2. Add offal and cook for 10 minutes.
3. Add cabbage and chives, simmering until tender.
4. Serve hot.

Yakiimo (Roasted Sweet Potatoes)

Ingredients

- 2 Japanese sweet potatoes (satsumaimo)

Instructions

1. Preheat oven to 375°F (190°C).
2. Wash and dry sweet potatoes, then place them on a baking sheet.
3. Bake for 45–60 minutes until soft.
4. Serve hot.

Fugu Nabe (Blowfish Hot Pot)

Ingredients

- 4 cups fugu (blowfish) broth
- 200g fugu fillet, sliced
- 1/2 cup mushrooms
- 1/2 cup tofu, cubed
- 1/4 cup napa cabbage
- 1 tbsp soy sauce

Instructions

1. Simmer fugu broth with soy sauce.
2. Add fish, mushrooms, tofu, and cabbage.
3. Cook for 5 minutes until fish is done.
4. Serve hot.

Kamameshi (Iron Pot Rice)

Ingredients

- 1 cup short-grain rice
- 1 1/2 cups dashi broth
- 1/2 cup chicken, diced
- 1/4 cup mushrooms, sliced
- 1 tbsp soy sauce
- 1 tbsp mirin

Instructions

1. Rinse rice and add to an iron pot with dashi, soy sauce, and mirin.
2. Add chicken and mushrooms.
3. Cover and cook on low heat for 20 minutes.
4. Let sit for 5 minutes before serving.

Kinoko Gohan (Mushroom Rice)

Ingredients

- 1 cup short-grain rice
- 1 1/2 cups dashi broth
- 1/2 cup mixed mushrooms (shiitake, enoki, maitake)
- 1 tbsp soy sauce
- 1 tbsp mirin

Instructions

1. Rinse rice and add to a pot with dashi, soy sauce, and mirin.
2. Add mushrooms and cook on low heat for 20 minutes.
3. Let sit for 5 minutes before serving.

Hokkaido Butter Corn Ramen (Creamy Corn Ramen)

Ingredients

- 3 cups chicken broth
- 1 tbsp miso paste
- 1 tbsp butter
- 1/2 cup corn kernels
- 200g ramen noodles

Instructions

1. Simmer chicken broth with miso paste.
2. Cook ramen noodles and serve in the broth.
3. Top with butter and corn.

Zōsui (Rice Porridge from Hot Pot Broth)

Ingredients

- 2 cups leftover hot pot broth
- 1/2 cup cooked rice
- 1 egg, beaten
- 1/4 cup green onions, chopped
- 1/2 tsp soy sauce

Instructions

1. Bring hot pot broth to a simmer.
2. Add cooked rice and stir gently.
3. Slowly drizzle in beaten egg, stirring lightly.
4. Season with soy sauce and garnish with green onions.

Salmon Chan-Chan Yaki (Miso-Grilled Salmon)

Ingredients

- 2 salmon fillets
- 2 tbsp miso paste
- 1 tbsp soy sauce
- 1 tbsp mirin
- 1/2 cup cabbage, shredded
- 1/2 cup mushrooms, sliced

Instructions

1. Mix miso, soy sauce, and mirin into a marinade.
2. Spread marinade over salmon fillets.
3. Grill salmon with cabbage and mushrooms until cooked through.

Hiyayakko (Cold Tofu with Toppings)

Ingredients

- 1 block silken tofu
- 1 tbsp soy sauce
- 1 tbsp grated ginger
- 1 tbsp chopped green onions
- 1/2 tbsp bonito flakes (optional)

Instructions

1. Cut tofu into small cubes.
2. Top with ginger, green onions, and bonito flakes.
3. Drizzle with soy sauce before serving.

Anago Meshi (Grilled Saltwater Eel Rice)

Ingredients

- 1 grilled anago (saltwater eel) fillet
- 1 bowl cooked rice
- 1 tbsp eel sauce (unagi tare)
- 1/2 tbsp green onions, chopped

Instructions

1. Slice grilled anago into thin strips.
2. Serve eel over rice and drizzle with eel sauce.
3. Garnish with green onions.

Gindara Saikyo Yaki (Miso-Marinated Black Cod)

Ingredients

- 2 black cod fillets
- 2 tbsp white miso paste
- 1 tbsp mirin
- 1 tbsp sake
- 1 tsp sugar

Instructions

1. Mix miso, mirin, sake, and sugar into a marinade.
2. Coat cod fillets and marinate for 24 hours.
3. Grill until golden and caramelized.

Tofu Steak (Pan-Seared Tofu in Sauce)

Ingredients

- 1 block firm tofu, sliced into thick pieces
- 1 tbsp soy sauce
- 1 tbsp mirin
- 1/2 tbsp sesame oil
- 1 tbsp cornstarch

Instructions

1. Coat tofu slices lightly with cornstarch.
2. Pan-sear in sesame oil until golden.
3. Add soy sauce and mirin, simmering briefly before serving.

Oyakodon (Chicken and Egg Rice Bowl)

Ingredients

- 1/2 cup chicken thigh, sliced
- 1/4 cup onion, sliced
- 1/2 cup dashi broth
- 1 tbsp soy sauce
- 1 tbsp mirin
- 1 egg, beaten
- 1 bowl cooked rice

Instructions

1. Simmer dashi, soy sauce, mirin, and onion in a pan.
2. Add chicken and cook until done.
3. Pour in beaten egg and let it set slightly.
4. Serve over rice.

Takikomi Gohan (Seasoned Mixed Rice)

Ingredients

- 1 cup short-grain rice
- 1 1/2 cups dashi broth
- 1/4 cup shiitake mushrooms, sliced
- 1/4 cup carrots, julienned
- 1 tbsp soy sauce
- 1 tbsp mirin

Instructions

1. Rinse rice and place in a pot with dashi, soy sauce, and mirin.
2. Add mushrooms and carrots.
3. Cook on low heat for 20 minutes.
4. Let sit for 5 minutes before serving.

Buri Daikon (Simmered Yellowtail and Daikon)

Ingredients

- 2 yellowtail (buri) fillets
- 1/2 cup daikon, sliced
- 1 cup dashi broth
- 2 tbsp soy sauce
- 1 tbsp mirin
- 1 tsp sugar

Instructions

1. Simmer dashi, soy sauce, mirin, and sugar in a pot.
2. Add daikon and cook until soft.
3. Add yellowtail and simmer for 10 minutes.
4. Serve warm.

Nikuman (Steamed Meat Buns)

Ingredients

- 2 cups all-purpose flour
- 1/2 cup warm water
- 1 tsp yeast
- 1 tbsp sugar
- 100g ground pork
- 1/4 cup onion, minced
- 1 tbsp soy sauce
- 1 tsp ginger, grated

Instructions

1. Mix warm water, yeast, and sugar. Let sit for 10 minutes.
2. Add flour and knead into a smooth dough. Let rise for 1 hour.
3. Mix pork, onion, soy sauce, and ginger.
4. Divide dough into small pieces, fill with meat mixture, and seal.
5. Steam for 15 minutes until fluffy.

Yosenabe (Mixed Hot Pot)

Ingredients

- 4 cups dashi broth
- 200g thinly sliced meat (chicken, beef, or pork)
- 1/2 cup tofu, cubed
- 1/2 cup mushrooms
- 1/2 cup napa cabbage
- 1 tbsp soy sauce

Instructions

1. Heat dashi broth in a pot.
2. Add meat, tofu, mushrooms, and cabbage.
3. Simmer until cooked and serve hot.

Imoni (Taro and Beef Stew)

Ingredients

- 4 cups dashi broth
- 200g beef, sliced
- 1/2 cup taro, peeled and cubed
- 1/2 cup konnyaku, sliced
- 1 tbsp soy sauce
- 1 tbsp mirin

Instructions

1. Simmer dashi broth with soy sauce and mirin.
2. Add taro and konnyaku, cooking until tender.
3. Add beef and cook for 5 minutes.

Tamago Zake (Egg and Sake Drink)

Ingredients

- 1 cup sake
- 1 egg
- 1 tbsp honey

Instructions

1. Warm sake in a pot (do not boil).
2. Whisk egg and honey together.
3. Slowly pour warm sake into the egg mixture, stirring constantly.
4. Serve immediately.

Kiritanpo (Grilled Rice Skewers)

Ingredients

- 2 cups cooked rice
- 1/2 tsp salt
- 4 wooden skewers

Instructions

1. Mash rice and mix with salt.
2. Shape rice around skewers and press firmly.
3. Grill over an open flame until golden brown.

Satsuma Jiru (Pork and Sweet Potato Soup)

Ingredients

- 4 cups dashi broth
- 200g pork belly, sliced
- 1/2 cup sweet potatoes, diced
- 1/2 cup miso paste
- 1/4 cup green onions

Instructions

1. Simmer dashi broth and miso paste.
2. Add pork and sweet potatoes, cooking until tender.
3. Garnish with green onions.

Kinako Mochi (Toasted Soybean Flour-Covered Mochi)

Ingredients

- 2 mochi pieces
- 1/4 cup kinako (roasted soybean flour)
- 1 tbsp sugar

Instructions

1. Toast mochi until puffy.
2. Mix kinako and sugar, then coat mochi before serving.

Anmitsu (Winter Dessert with Red Beans and Jelly)

Ingredients

- 1/2 cup kanten (agar jelly), cubed
- 1/4 cup sweet red beans (anko)
- 1/2 cup fresh fruit (strawberries, mandarin oranges)
- 1 tbsp kuromitsu (brown sugar syrup)

Instructions

1. Arrange kanten, red beans, and fruit in a bowl.
2. Drizzle with kuromitsu before serving.

Yuba Soba (Tofu Skin Soba Noodles)

Ingredients

- 2 cups dashi broth
- 1 tbsp soy sauce
- 1 tsp mirin
- 200g soba noodles
- 1/4 cup yuba (tofu skin)

Instructions

1. Simmer dashi broth with soy sauce and mirin.
2. Cook soba noodles and add to the broth.
3. Top with yuba before serving.

Hakusai Itame (Stir-Fried Napa Cabbage)

Ingredients

- 2 cups napa cabbage, chopped
- 1 tbsp soy sauce
- 1 tsp sesame oil
- 1/2 tsp garlic, minced

Instructions

1. Heat sesame oil in a pan.
2. Stir-fry garlic and cabbage until tender.
3. Add soy sauce and cook for 1 more minute.

Dorayaki (Red Bean Pancakes)

Ingredients

- 1 cup all-purpose flour
- 1/2 cup sugar
- 1/2 tsp baking powder
- 2 eggs
- 1/2 cup water
- 1/2 cup sweet red bean paste (anko)

Instructions

1. Mix flour, sugar, baking powder, eggs, and water into a batter.
2. Cook small pancakes on a non-stick pan until golden.
3. Spread red bean paste between two pancakes and serve.